Simeon & the Purple Pearl

Written & Illustrated by

Jennifer Maska

Simeon and the Purple Pearl

Original story and artwork by Jennifer Maska
Book design and layout by Joshua Muster, Creative Alternatives Press
Creative Alternatives Press is a wholly owned imprint of HBE Publishing. www.hbepublishing.com

Orders, inquiries, and correspondence should be addressed to:

Jennifer Maska
lecopeland372@gmail.com

Printed in November 2015 in the USA

Hardback ISBN 978-1-943050-19-2

Creative Alternatives Press

Clovis, California

Thanks to my sisters Doreen, Maria and Linda for their advice and encouragement in making this book, and to my friend Michael for letting me use his computer.

Kneeling by the seashore, a robed man of 33 years named Jesus was sifting sand between his fingers. It fell into the water and floated near a clam named Chloe, where upon a certain grain got caught in her shell.

Imagine how you would feel if you had a grain of sand in your eye!

The newly implanted grain caused a strange reaction inside Chloe's body. Her personality started changing. She was no longer clammy and aloof. She said, "God is love! Whoever lives in love lives in God, and God in him! The key is to love others as yourself!"

OVER TIME, THE IMPLANTED GRAIN IN HER BODY GREW AND GREW TO BE A LARGE PURPLE PEARL. YOU MIGHT SAY IT WAS A DIVINE DISTURBANCE.

Often, schools of fish would listen to Chloe as she shared the good news that Jesus, or Yeshua, saves!

Freddy and Francine the flying fish talked about Chloe's message.

"Chloe said Jesus saves!" said Freddy.

"He's the Son of God and saves us from our sins!" said Francine.

THE MOTHER WHALE SANG TO HER BABY . . .

THE STARFISH DANCED AND THE JELLYFISH SWIRLED AND TWIRLED . . .

THE KISSING FISH KISSED . . .

THE SEASQUIRTS SMILED . . .

THE DOLPHINS LEAPED FROM THE WATER WITH JOY!

The crabs clicked their pinchers and the turtles flapped their feet . . .

THE ORCA DIVED HAPPILY THROUGH THE SEAWEED!

The barracudas smiled their toothy grins . . .

As did the sharks . . .

THE SEAHORSES CURLED THEIR TAILS . . .

THE SAIL FISH UNFURLED HIS SAIL AND FLASHED HIS SPEAR NOSE . . .

THE MANTA RAYS GLIDED FOR JOY!

THE ANGEL FISH, GOLD FISH, EELS AND MOLLUSKS WERE ALL DELIGHTED!

From far and wide, many sea creatures came to listen to Chloe and her message.

One day Chloe met a seamonkey named Simeon. They became best friends and shared many adventures together!

One such adventure was when they discovered some under water geysers and jumped onto them to ride the bubble jets! They returned to the geysers to play for many days.

One day, Simeon told his friend Chloe that he didn't feel like playing on the geysers.

"What's wrong? Why are you so sad?" Chloe asked.

Simeon replied, "My mom is sick and Doctor Octopus is examining her and Meriah the mermaid is caring for her."

Simeon grew to be good friends with Meriah, especially since Meriah was caring for his mom.

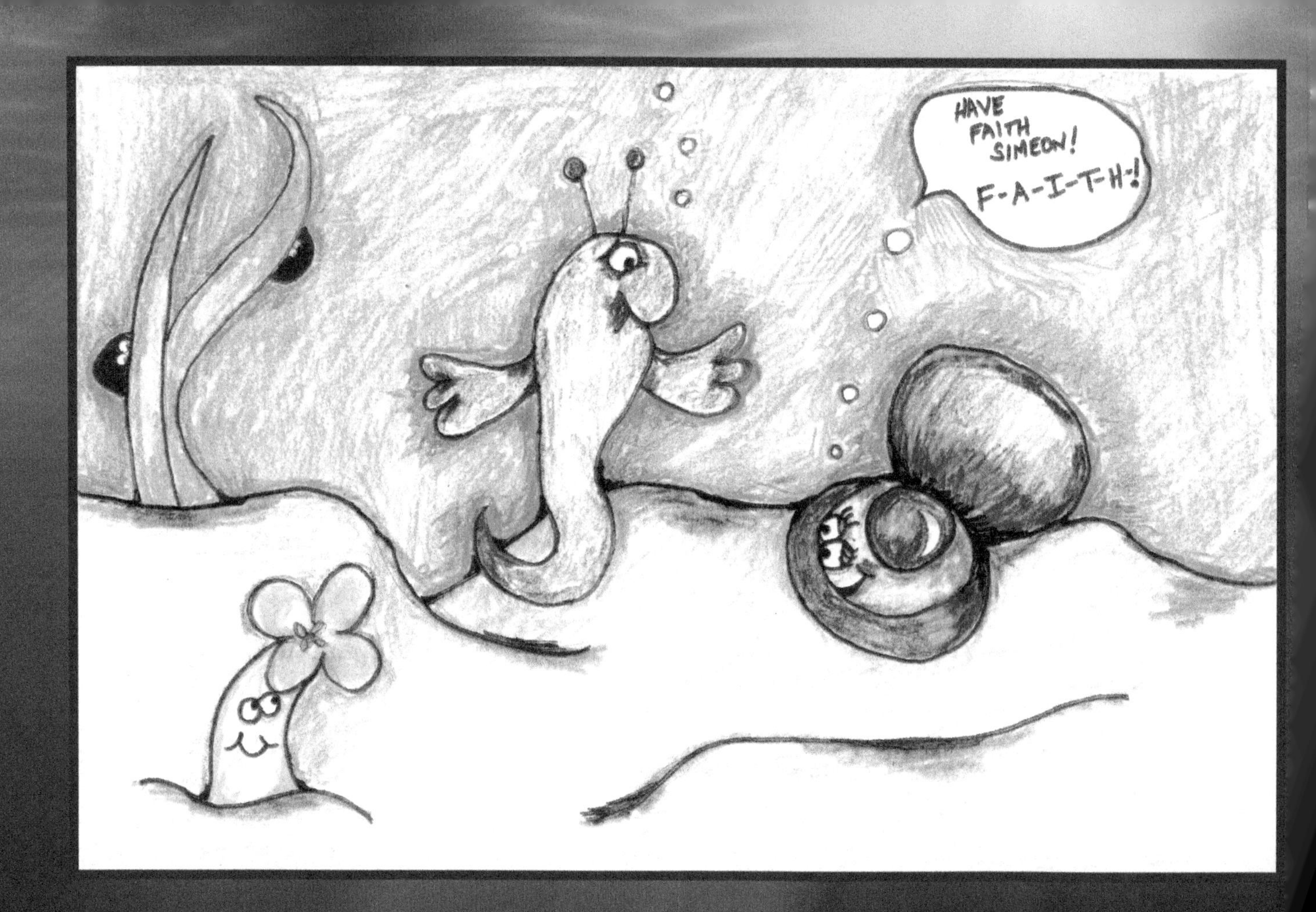

Chloe told Simeon to have faith that God would help his mother recover.

SIMEON'S MOM RECOVERED AND HE WAS GRATEFUL TO HIS FRIENDS CHLOE AND MERIAH FOR THEIR SUPPORT.

Meriah learned from Simeon about Chloe and her purple pearl and asked Simeon if Chloe would show it to her.

One sunny summer day, Simeon went looking for his friend CHloe. He went to all the usual places and finally found her abondoned shell with the purple pearl nearby.

"Oh my friend Chloe!" cried Simeon. "Has the Lord called you home? What shall I do?"

Alone in his grief, he heard a whisper and thought of Meriah who had wanted to see the pearl.

"Pass it on . . ." the voice whispered to him.

Simeon decided to give that purple pearl and its message to his friend Meriah who so wanted to see it!

The purple pearl is very precious because it represents the gospel of Jesus Christ.

Chloe and Simeon had shared the good news that Jesus saves with all creation under the sea!

The gospel message of the purple pearl: Jesus Christ is the son of our living God. He died for our sins and rose from the grave to interceed to Father God for his children and promises everlasting life to all those that love him!

Have some fun and get a big box of crayons and color the following pictures!

CPSIA information can be obtained
at www.ICGtesting.com
Printed in the USA
LVOW05*0337131215
466094LV00013B/15/P

9 781943 05